William the Conqueror

WHO WAS...

William the
Conqueror

The Norman King

CHARLOTTE
MOORE

Illustrations by Alex Fox

✳ SHORT BOOKS

First published in 2006 by

Short Books

3A Exmouth House

Pine Street, London EC1R 0JH

10 9 8 7 6 5 4 3 2 1

A CIP catalogue record for this book
is available from the British Library.

Illustration copyright © Alex Fox 2006

Quiz copyright © Sebastian Blake

ISBN 1-904977-61-8

Printed in Great Britain by
Bookmarque Ltd, Croydon, Surrey

To my parents, who brought me up in 1066 country

Prologue
The Bayeux Tapestry

" Sister Cecilia! Your hands are idle. How may Bishop Odo's tapestry be ready in time if you sit gazing out of the window? The great cathedral at Bayeux is to be dedicated in July, as well you know. Already it is April, and much remains to be done."

Sister Cecilia stifled a small sigh. She knew there was justice in the Mother Superior's rebuke. Cecilia was the youngest of the nuns to be allowed to work on the great embroidery that told the tale of William's victory and Harold's defeat, and she felt the honour keenly. But through the round-arched windows of the long chamber she could glimpse the orchard, watch the rosy-breasted bull finches swinging in the fruit trees, gobbling the fat buds. She could hear the shrill cries of the little boy who was paid a penny a day to drive them away. And that morning, for the first time this year, she had heard the cuckoo's call, as haunting as an echo in the depths of the burgeoning wood.

The bursting blossom and the rising sap summoned her, stirred her blood. But she had dedicated her life to God, and one of the vows she had taken was the vow of obedience. She must put aside the springtime pleasures of her early childhood – gathering honey-scented cowslips in the dew-drenched pastures; discovering a thrushes' nest, each egg a miniature blue sky. She must bow her head over her sewing, as the other nuns did. She must ply her needle, tug the coloured wool through the strong linen until her fingers ached.

And she knew her work was very fine. She hoped it was not a sin of pride to think that. She was aware that she had been chosen for the task in preference to other, more experienced nuns, because under her nimble fingers the animals and plants that decorated the borders of the great embroidery flickered into life. She had no part in the grand design – that had been entrusted to an artist, a man of course, not a humble nun. But Cecilia and the other seamstresses were allowed a little freedom with the details, and she loved to create dogs, horses, deer, weasels, birds with fantastical plumage, even magical creatures like gryphons and dragons, to writhe and strut and squabble round the edges of the main story.

And what a story it was! Cecilia had been entrusted with the lion's share of the work on one of the most important scenes. This scene was the turning point of the terrible Battle of Hastings. The invading Norman troops were losing heart. A rumour flew through the ranks that Duke William had been killed. Heedless of danger, the Duke had removed his helmet to reveal his face, and then he galloped in front of his men, brandishing his lance, shouting "Look at me, I am alive, and by God's help I shall win."

And win he did. Cecilia's heart swelled with admiration. She had been only six years old at the time of the battle, but she remembered how people talked of it, the tales of courage in the face of such horror, the descriptions of mangled corpses of men and horses lying in pools of blood. She remembered muttered conversations round her parents' fireside, her father cursing Duke William as a usurper who had stolen King Harold's crown. But even then, Cecilia did not share her father's indignation. To her, William was the rightful King of England, a hero who deserved high office.

The nuns had been told to expect a visit from Queen Mathilda any day now. The Queen had taken a lively interest in the embroidery right from the start, had already visited several times, and had even undertaken a little stitching herself. She would certainly want to inspect the important scene entrusted to Cecilia's care.

Cecilia gave herself a shake, and vowed to work harder. She had finished the russet loops of William's chainmail, finished the dull gold curves of his high-pommelled saddle, but she hesitated before starting on the face of the King himself. It was a daunting task. How could she, a girl of seventeen, record for all time the features of the Conqueror? For all time – these were the words the artist had impressed upon them. "This tapestry," he had declared, "is no mere decoration. A thousand years hence, men and women will marvel at the tale it has to tell of the greatest events in the history of our land."

A thousand years! Cecilia could not imagine it. Would not the world have ended by then? Already, the earth seemed ancient to her, weary beneath its spring dressing of lively green. But the artist was a clever man, he knew what he was about. Cecilia and the other nuns were helping him to shape history, to think about what had happened in a certain way. And that way was to the glory of King William, and to the detriment of the defeated Harold, struck down by an arrow in his eye.

A murmur rippled through the chamber like the wind in long grass. "The Queen is here!" Every nun bent still lower over her work. Cecilia sensed, rather than saw, the tiny figure, no bigger than a child but straight-backed and dignified, followed by her ladies-in-waiting. Mathilda had been married to William for 27 years and had borne him nine children, but her steady step and regal bearing belied the weight of her years.

The royal group moved from one section of the tapestry to another, full of comments and exclamations, criticism as well as praise. When the Queen halted next to the frame on which Cecilia's section was stretched, Cecilia bowed in homage, as she had been trained to do. As she rose, she shot a daring glance at the visitors. Their coloured gowns looked so delicious, after the plain vestments of the nuns! Mathilda herself wore a robe of mossy green, the wide sleeves trimmed with rose-pink, silk ribbon. Her ladies-in-waiting were decked in blues and greens and purples, gorgeous as a cockerel's plumage in sunlight.

"I remember you," said the Queen, placing her small hand lightly on Cecilia's shoulder. "On my last visit, you were working on a greyhound chasing a hare; I well remember the way the hare bounded away from the hound, leaping almost out of the frame. Am I right, Sister?"

"Yes, indeed, your Majesty," replied Cecilia, her fair Saxon skin flushing pink with pleasure at being remembered by so great a personage.

"Tell me your name, girl."

"I am Sister Cecilia, your Majesty."

"Cecilia! An excellent choice of name, for it is the name of my daughter, who dedicated her life to God when she was only seven years old. My Cecilia is a wise and pious woman, girl. May you live to follow her example."

Cecilia murmured an "Amen," and made the sign of the cross. Gratified, Mathilda turned her attention to the work in hand. "Ah! The thick of the battle! This is Bishop Odo, with his wand of office. And this, if I mistake not, is my own husband. But as yet, he has no head."

"Not yet, your majesty. He raises his helmet to rally the troops, and …"

"Excuse me, Sister. I need to take your place a while."

The Queen lowered herself onto the work bench. She snapped her fingers, and her attendants brought cushions to raise her up – she really was as tiny as a child of nine. She selected a needle and threaded it.

"You will not take it amiss, Cecilia, if I complete the King's face? After all, who knows it better than I?"

Cecilia lowered her head. "It would be a great

13

honour, madame."

The Queen worked quickly. She completed not only the head, but the hands as well, one raising the visor, the other brandishing a club. Her William was heavy-browed, strong-jawed, imposing. The work done, she rose with a sigh.

"He had three horses shot from under him that day," she said, as if to herself, "Yet still he led his troops to victory. My husband is a proper man!"

Cecilia and the waiting-women murmured assent. As the Queen turned to go, she clasped the girl's hands in her own. Cecilia could feel her hard-edged rings pressing into her flesh.

"You will never forget me," declared Mathilda, "And your little fingers have helped to make sure that the world will never forget my husband. This tapestry will proclaim the glory of William I, Duke of Normandy and Conqueror of England, for all time!"

For all time! Those words again. Cecilia sank to her knees, and kissed the Queen's hands. "Amen to that, your Majesty," she whispered, with an overflowing heart.

CHAPTER ONE
THE BOY DUKE

Everyone has heard of William the Conqueror, but no one knows exactly when he was born. It may have been in the autumn of 1027, or early in 1028. We do know that he was born at Falaise, a town in Normandy. Normandy is part of France now, but in those days it was a separate country.

William's father was Robert, Duke of Normandy. He was the most powerful man in Normandy, which made him one of the most powerful rulers in Europe. His nickname was "The Magnificent"; he was feared and respected.

William's mother, Herleva, however, was not from

a grand family. Her father was either a tanner or an undertaker, or possibly both. Tanners work with animal skins, turning them into leather. Undertakers prepare dead bodies for burial. Both jobs were considered lowly and unclean. The young William was teased about his mother's "dirty" family. Many years later, in 1051, when William as Duke of Normandy attacked the town of Alençon, some of its citizens taunted him by beating animal skins and furs in front of him. William ordered that the hands and feet of his tormentors should be sliced off. No one dared to tease him about his mother's family again.

Herleva was of humble origin, but her graceful dancing attracted the attention of Duke Robert. He fell in love with the pretty young girl and set up home with her, but he never married her. This meant that William was illegitimate, a "bastard". William hated to be reminded of this. All his life he struggled to prove that a "bastard" could be as powerful, if not more powerful, than any man born legitimate.

Though Duke Robert didn't marry William's mother he was proud of his young son. He acknowledged him as his heir and made the other noblemen swear an oath of loyalty to him. Right from the start, everyone felt that William was a remarkable boy. When Herleva had been pregnant with him she had dreamed that her insides were stretched out to cover the whole of Normandy and England. Later this dream was seen as a foreshadowing of William's conquest of England. And it was said that on the day William was born he seized the cut rushes that covered the floor of the chamber and shook them with his tiny hands.

While his father lived, William's childhood was happy and secure. But in 1035, Duke Robert set off on a pilgrimage to visit the sacred places in the Holy Land. From Jerusalem he sent back the fingerbone of St Stephen. This was an important relic; in those days most people believed that saints' relics could work miracles. But St Stephen's bone didn't help Duke Robert. On the return journey he became ill and died. Could he have been poisoned by his enemies? In those harsh times, that was a strong possibility.

Now William was Duke of Normandy, although he was only seven or eight years old. Immediately, Normandy was plunged into civil war, because the feuding noblemen no longer had Duke Robert to control them. Young William had little power. He was looked after by two guardians who made most of his decisions for him, but they were both murdered after a time. William's young life was often in danger. His uncle Walter, his mother's brother, slept in William's bedroom to guard him, and often hid him in the cottages of poor people where his enemies wouldn't think of looking for him.

William's life was now dominated by fear and danger, which had a profound effect on him. From that time on, he was always on the alert, never relaxed. He was by nature brave and strong; now he became cruel. His cruelty should not surprise us – all around him he saw violence, and it became normal to him.

After Duke Robert's death, Herleva married a minor nobleman called Count Herluin de Conteville. They had two sons, Odo, and Robert of Mortain. These boys were William's half-brothers, and it seems that his mother's new family gave William some kind of security. Later, he gave Odo and Robert very important jobs and showered them with money, castles and land. They in their turn were his most valued supporters, at least until he quarrelled bitterly with Odo, but that was when they were both middle-aged.

William didn't get much in the way of an education. He didn't go to school and probably never learned to read or write, but that wasn't unusual in the eleventh century, even for a Duke. With a few exceptions, the only people who could read and write were priests and monks. But William was taught to be a good soldier. He became an excellent horseman, skilled in the use of weapons. He enjoyed learning these techniques with other aristocratic boys of his own age; he adored hunting, archery and swordplay.

As William grew older he began to assert his control over his Dukedom of Normandy. The quarrelsome nobles, who had thought they could get away with anything when they had had a mere child as their ruler, came to realise that the child was fast becoming a powerful, intelligent, ruthless man. William grew very tall. He was five foot ten inches (1.75 metres) which was very unusual for those days, when most people were much shorter than they are now. He was extremely strong, and proud of his strength. He could draw a bow which other men couldn't even bend while spurring on a warhorse at the same time – a great feat of strength and control. We don't know much about what he looked like, but we do know that he was cleanshaven, his dark hair was cut short, and that his voice was harsh and rough. He became a formidable man. People had no choice but to respect Duke William.

Once he had reached manhood and managed his dukedom alone, without guardians, his main job was to keep his hostile neighbours under control. Normandy was subjected to constant raids from other provinces, such as Maine to the south and Brittany to the west. William led many attacks on his enemies and gained a reputation as a great general. He maintained good discipline in his army and was revered by his men.

He showed good judgement, for instance in 1057, at the Battle of Varaville. William shadowed his enemies, refraining from action until the time was right. The enemy troops were crossing the estuary of the Dives river near Varaville. William waited until the oncoming tide had split the army, then he pounced and shattered the rearguard. This victory was a landmark in William's fortunes. After Varaville, Normandy was never again invaded during his lifetime.

But, above all, William inspired awe and loyalty in his troops by his personal example of courage and energy. Once, when one of his uncles rebelled against his rule, William led a troop of horsemen to take him prisoner and rode so hard that the horses of his companions dropped from exhaustion. Time and time again, William's horses were killed under him in battle (three in the Battle of Hastings itself), but he always remounted and carried on. And, though William was harsh and cruel to his enemies, he was fair, even generous, to his soldiers and supporters. The people of Normandy soon came to realise that they had never had a more effective leader than Duke William.

William knew he should marry. He wanted a wife to support him and to bear him children who would become his heirs. He chose Mathilda, the daughter of

Count Baldwin of Flanders. This was an advantageous match for William — Baldwin's family was one of the most noble in Europe. Mathilda was proud of her aristocratic ancestry. By marrying her, William hoped to wipe away the stain of his own illegitimacy.

And he had chosen well from other points of view. Mathilda was tiny, perhaps only four foot three inches tall (1.29 metres), but she was clever, talented and tough. William spent a lot of time travelling; he made Mathilda his Regent, leaving her to rule in his absence, and she made a good job of it. They had nine children, four boys and five girls. The children were all strong and healthy, and several of them reached old age. This was remarkable in an era when disease was rife and medicine very crude.

William and Mathilda had great respect for one another. Unlike other rulers of his time, William was a faithful husband and didn't keep a mistress. They were both deeply religious. Together, they set about building churches and abbeys throughout Normandy. They chose the city of Caen as their favourite town. At Caen, William founded the Abbey of St. Etienne (St. Stephen), and here he placed the sacred fingerbone of St. Stephen in memory of his father. Mathilda founded the sister abbey of La Trinité. Both wanted to be buried in these special places. They developed Caen as a centre of learning and religion. They must have found great pleasure and satisfaction, working together on these ambitious projects.

Their first son, Robert, was born soon after their marriage. William named Robert as heir to the Duchy of Normandy and made the nobles swear the oath of loyalty to him. The next son was Richard, then William, then Henry who was by far the youngest. Years later, Richard died in a hunting accident. William, whose nickname was William Rufus because he had red hair and a red face – 'rufus' is the Latin word for red – eventually succeeded his father as King of England. His younger brother Henry also became King of England, since Rufus died without a son.

Much less is known about the five girls – indeed, there may even have been more than five. We can't be sure of all their names or the order in which they were born, but it seems likely that there were Adelida, Cecilia, Mathilda, Constance and Adela. The one we know most about is Cecilia, who entered her mother's abbey of La Trinité to train to be a nun at the age of only seven. Cecilia grew up to become Abbess of La Trinité. She lived to a great age, and was widely admired for her scholarship and strength of character.

Later, William's family life would be marred by quarrels, particularly with his oldest son Robert. But in the early years William was proud of his large brood of healthy children and of his capable and loyal wife. He had strengthened the power of Normandy and succeeded in keeping his enemies under control. He had come a long way from the perils and insults of his childhood. And to cap it all, Edward the Confessor, the childless King of England, had nominated William as heir to the English throne – or so William chose to believe. The present was good. The future looked rosier still.

CHAPTER TWO
HAROLD AND WILLIAM — FRIENDS AND RIVALS

William relished the thought that one day he might be King of England as well as Duke of Normandy, but he knew he was not the only man to dream of sitting on the English throne. King Edward, nicknamed "The Confessor" because of his deep interest in religion, was married, but he had no children to succeed him. There were several younger men who could lay claim to the throne after his death, and the choice was not King Edward's alone. A group of advisers, called the "Witan", also had a say in the matter.

King Edward was a cousin of William's father, Duke Robert. This blood tie put William in the running. Besides, Edward was impressed by what he knew of the young Duke of Normandy. England had not been a united country for very long. For years, the Vikings had controlled large areas, especially in the North of England, and even now there were frequent threats of invasion from Norway and Denmark. Edward was worried that his fragile kingdom might fall apart after his death. He needed a strong, intelligent man to succeed him, and William of Normandy was shaping up nicely.

It seems likely that William visited England for the first time when he was 24 years old, and that during this visit he got to know Edward the Confessor and gained his respect. Kind Edward spoke English, but his first language was Norman French, so he probably enjoyed discussing politics with William in his mother tongue. As a result, Edward nominated William as his heir. But Edward should not have made this announcement without consulting the Witan; so many people saw the nomination as invalid. Taking matters into his own hands meant that he was laying down trouble for the future.

The other main claimant to the English throne was Harold Godwinson, son of the redoubtable Godwin, Earl of Essex. The Godwins were the most powerful family in England. Harold's sister Edith was married to Edward the Confessor. Their mother, Gytha, gave birth to at least six other children, of whom Swein, Tostig, Leofwine and Gyrth were all important English earls who owned large tracts of land. The Godwins held sway at the heart of English politics.

Harold was about five years older than William of Normandy. His earldom stretched across East Anglia, Essex, Huntingdonshire and Cambridgeshire. In his early twenties he fell in love with a rich and beautiful girl, Edith, nicknamed Swanneshals (Swan-neck) on account of her long and graceful neck. Harold didn't marry Edith, but he set her up in one of his manor houses and visited her often. The couple had five children and were close and happy. This arrangement was quite usual; it was called a "Danish marriage". It left an important man like Harold free to make a politically advantageous marriage at a later date if a suitable bride came along, and this is what

Harold eventually did.

Harold was in fact Earl Godwin's second son – he became the heir when his elder brother Swein disgraced himself, first by abducting the Abbess of Leominster and then by murdering a cousin. Swein was declared a "nithing", a disgraced outcast, and forced into exile.

When Harold was 30, Godwin died. The story goes that the earl was feasting at a banquet at Winchester. He had been accused of a murder that had happened some twenty years before, and cried, "May the Lord strike me down if I am guilty," where upon he choked on a fishbone and died.

Harold succeeded to his father's title and to his immense wealth – the Godwin family was richer than the King himself. He also became King Edward's deputy, the second most important man in government. Harold was a more educated man than William. He delighted in the exquisite painted and jewelled books produced by monks – in those days, before the invention of printing, all books were written by hand, so they were extremely precious. Harold also travelled more widely than William. He visited Bruges, Germany, Denmark, France and Italy. He had long fair hair and a thick yellow moustache. Like William, he was physically strong and brave.

But he was a much friendlier, more likeable man than his rival. Harold could be fierce and tough, and he accompanied other members of his family on piratical raids during which slaves were taken, but he was without William's streak of cold cruelty. He enjoyed gambling, drinking and playing dice, and was extremely popular amongst his men, who regarded him as a hero.

In 1064, Harold sailed to Normandy. Was he sent there by Edward the Confessor, carrying a message to confirm William as the English heir? If so, he must have set sail with a heavy heart. Or – as seems more likely – perhaps the purpose of his journey was to negotiate the release of his brother Wulfnoth and nephew Hakon who were both being held hostage in Normandy.

Whatever the reason, Harold's voyage had far-reaching consequences. A storm blew up, his ship was wrecked, and Harold and his men were washed up on the shore. They were quickly surrounded by a ring of soldiers who took them as prisoners to their master, Count Guy of Ponthieu. Guy locked Harold in his dungeon – he hoped to gain a large sum of money as a ransom.

Duke William heard the news. He was curious to meet this famous Englishman face to face, so he arranged his release through a mixture of bribery and threat. William took Harold to his castle of Bonneville and treated him as an honoured guest. Duchess Mathilda liked Harold, who was easy, cheerful company. There was even talk of Harold marrying her eldest daughter, who was still only a child. Harold joined William on some of his military expeditions, and on one occasion Harold with his own hands rescued some Norman knights who were sinking into a quicksand.

Harold passed several months pleasantly enough as the guest of William and Mathilda. But as time went on he began to realise that he wasn't a guest so much as a prisoner, albeit in grand and comfortable surroundings. Harold wanted to return to England, but William wasn't going to let him leave until he'd got what he wanted from him. What did William want?

He wanted Harold to swear an oath of allegiance, to promise to support William's claim to the English throne when Edward the Confessor died. If Harold swore the oath, then in return William said he would arrange the release of Wulfnoth and Hakon (a promise he did not fulfil).

Trapped in William's castle, Harold decided that he would take the oath in order to escape. At the back of his mind was the idea that some oaths were easily broken. But William made him swear with his hand on a wooden box. It was only afterwards that Harold discovered what the box contained – bones of saints, and other holy relics.

Harold, like William, was a religious man, and he took these things seriously. He worried that God would punish him if he broke his vow to support William. A few years earlier, Harold had been crippled by paralysis in his leg. He had prayed to God, God had cured him, and to show his gratitude Harold had built an abbey at Waltham Cross, a very special place for him, and the place where he wanted to be buried. Harold was terrified of angering God. Besides, if Harold went on to accept the English

crown having sworn on the holy relics, his sister Queen Edith, an extremely pious woman, would regard him as an outcast of the church.

It was all most unsatisfactory. Harold went home with his mind in turmoil. He had plenty of problems to deal with back in England. His brother Tostig was causing trouble. Tostig was an unstable character who bore a lot of grudges. He was Earl of Northumbria, but he was deeply unpopular. The thegns, the name given to the leaders in villages in

England at the time, were rebelling against him. They wanted to replace him with a man named Morcar. Harold, who couldn't trust his brother, struck a deal with Morcar, and Tostig was driven into exile. It may seem unkind of Harold to turn against his brother, but he had good reason. Once, staying at Hereford, Tostig had murdered Harold's servants as the result of a quarrel, and had departed leaving a contemptuous message for Harold that he had had the servants' bodies pickled to keep him in food for the winter.

King Edward was growing older and more frail. His health had never been strong; surely his death could not be far off? Realising that a suitable wife and a legitimate son would strengthen his chances of becoming king, Harold quickly married Ealdgyth, sister of his new Northumbrian ally Morcar. They soon produced a baby son, Harold Haroldson. What Edith Swan-neck thought of this arrangement can only be guessed at, but it was to her and not to his new wife that Harold bade his last farewell before the Battle of Hastings.

King Edward died at dawn on January 5th, 1066. It seems that on his deathbed he changed his mind about his successor and favoured Harold over William. Perhaps he was too ill to care any more, or perhaps he had been bullied into nominating William in the first place. The English nobles who made up the Witan lost no time in proclaiming Harold the new king. He was anointed by Stigand, the Archbishop of York, the very day after Edward died.

Silver pennies bearing Harold's face were issued at once from more than forty mints. This was one way of confirming to the people of England that Harold was indeed their king. For years the English had listened with wonder and amusement to tales of Harold's daring deeds; he was the popular choice. Hardly anybody in England wanted William to be king. Right away, William knew that if he wanted to press his claim as rightful king of England, he had no choice but to invade.

Chapter Three
The Comet

"Hold her down, Alfred! Don't let her get away." Alfred did his best to obey his father, but the old ewe, struggling and terrified, was almost too much for his twelve-year-old strength. He sat on the close-cropped turf, nearer to the cliff's crumbling edge than he would have chosen, and gripped the sheep's head between his knees while with his hands he restrained her flailing forelegs.

Garth, Alfred's father, had been a shepherd all his life. He knew what he was doing. One lamb had already been born dead to this old ewe; its twin, stuck inside, would kill her if he didn't get it out.

Garth had greased his hands with the pig fat he stored in a stone jar in his shepherd's hut. He pressed his knees against the sheep's splayed hind legs to keep her pinioned on her back, then slipped an expert hand inside her.

"This one'll be dead, too," he grumbled. "It hasn't got a chance. It's this star. It brings bad news. The weather doesn't know whether it's Eastertide or Yule, the lambs are dying, and there was that two-headed calf born at Watt's farm last week. These are bad times, my son – dangerous times."

Alfred had heard all this before. For almost a week, a strange star had been observed, larger than most, cone-shaped, more flame-coloured than silver, and trailing a fiery tail that caused some folks to claim it was a dragon and no star at all. Such a sight was seen once in a lifetime, at most. It was an omen, all were agreed. But an omen for good or for ill?

And this late spring weather had been stranger than any could remember. Days of midsummer heat had been followed by frosts. There'd been rain-storms, too, and high winds that had whipped the sea into mountains and caverns grey as steel. The farmers were worried. The crops didn't know whether to sprout or not; the tender green shoots inched timid-ly forth, only to be blackened by frost or flattened by wind and hail.

Then there was that two-headed calf at Watt's place. True, nobody else had actually seen it, and Watt had the reputation as a teller of tall tales. Alfred and his best friend Ned, the miller's son, had plucked up the courage and walked the two miles inland to Watt's homestead, to ask if they could see the calf. No, said Watt, they couldn't. It had died, and he'd given it to his dogs. No sense wasting good meat. Now they'd best be off, he'd no time to waste in idle chatter with boys. Alfred and Ned, eyeing the tall shaggy hounds scratching their backs against the fence posts, were not inclined to linger.

The natural world was disturbed, but what did it all portend for England? Since the death of King Edward in January, Harold Godwinson had held the English throne. There were those who said the Saxon warrior hadn't enough royal blood in him to merit kingship, but his detractors were outnumbered by his supporters, who rejoiced in their strong and vigorous monarch, a welcome change after grey-bearded Edward – a holy man, no doubt, but a weak ruler. Everybody here on the south coast was braced for an invasion from France; the ambitions of Duke William of Normandy were well known. But a northern attack, from the Danes or the Norwegians, was just as likely.

Garth had named his son Alfred after the English king who had united the country. Were Alfred the Great's achievements all to be smashed to bits? Alfred wished he was old enough to fight. But if war broke out, his father would be summoned, and then he, too young to be a soldier, would have to manage the sheep and the pigs. This could happen any day. No one in England could feel safe, and this fantastical star fanned the flames of unease.

The old ewe had relaxed now. Alfred still held her tight, but her struggling had lessened to a few twitches; she seemed to sense that they were trying to help her. A grunt from Garth told Alfred that the job was nearly done. One tug, and his father pulled out his arm, streaked with blood to the elbow. A shiny bundle lay on the grass, hardly recognisable as a still-born lamb. "You can let her go now, son," said Garth, wiping his hands on the springy turf, but the exhausted ewe still lay on her side, panting.

"She'll be all right. Let's go. Carry the lamb, son The dogs'll have it."

Alfred hated to touch the dead thing, but he knew his father wanted to make a man of him. Squeamishness and tender feelings had no place in a shepherd's life. He suppressed a shudder as he bent over the slimy lump. But look — what was this? Movement, surely! The tiny creature was uncurling.

It stretched out a miniature front leg, then raised its head, wobbly on its skinny neck.

"Father! It's alive!"

"Now, who would have thought it?" Garth placed a restraining hand on his son's arm, for Alfred's instinct was to cradle the little survivor, let it share the warmth of his body. "We'll see if she'll take it, first. If we touch it, she won't know the smell. But if she won't take it, then we'll bring it to your mother." Elfrida, Alfred's mother, was expert at nursing orphaned lambs, helping them suck milk through a cone of sacking, keeping them warm in a straw-filled basket by the hearth.

Garth and Alfred stood back. The old ewe staggered to her feet. She began to nibble the grass, seemingly unaware of the presence of her baby. But then the lamb opened its mouth and uttered the faintest of bleats. The mother swung her heavy head in its direction. The lamb struggled to stand, but could only raise itself to it its knees before collapsing. The ewe moved towards it, nuzzled it, licked it clean of blood and slime, warmed it with her rasping tongue. At last, it was strong enough to raise itself and seek out her teat. As it began to suck, Alfred felt his eyes prick with tears.

Father and son stood watching in silence for a while. Then Garth ruffled his son's thick fair hair. "They're doing fine," he said. "We'll leave them to it."

As they made their way down the hillside, Alfred turned, and saw the ewe and lamb move on to join the rest of the flock. It felt like a miracle to him. One twin dead, the other sprung back to life! What did it all mean? What kind of an omen was that?

Chapter Four
The Fourteenth of October

The England to which both William and Harold laid claim had not been a united country for long. Until the tenth century, the kings of England had only really been kings of Wessex, in the south. Much of the rest was ruled by Danes and Norsemen, and even in 1066 the Danelaw still held sway in many parts. Scotland and Wales, of course, were still separate kingdoms, sometimes friendly towards England, sometimes hostile.

Whichever man won the English crown, his main job would be to strengthen England and to keep out invaders. In 1066 England had a population of one and a half to two million. London was by far the biggest city, with about 20,000 inhabitants. Other important cities were Winchester, which had been the capital when Alfred the Great was King of Wessex, and York, the northern stronghold.

Most people didn't live in towns or cities; they lived in small villages and worked on the land. Each large region was owned by an earl, who commanded troops from his area. Beneath the earls were the thegns, the top men in each village. At time of war, the thegns led the ordinary soldiers, under the command of the earls. In peacetime, the thegns oversaw all the village business and settled disputes. The thegns had quite a close and friendly relationship with the peasants, the ordinary people. After the Battle of Hastings this was to change; the higher ranks of the Norman conquerors started to shut themselves up in their castles and cut themselves off from the common people.

The bulk of the English army was called the Fyrd. One warrior from every five "hides" was called for service in the Fyrd – a hide was the landholding for one family. So, one family in five had to give up one of its menfolk to the Fyrd. But the men were only liable for two months' service at a time. After that, they could go back to ordinary life.

The army was swelled and strengthened by the housecarls, who had been introduced by King Canute. The housecarls were crack troops, well-trained, the king's own men. They were professional soldiers with a fearsome reputation.

As soon as he became king, Harold knew that he would have to keep his army on the alert. He suspected that William would plan an invasion, and he knew that his treacherous brother Tostig would cause trouble. From May until September 1066, Harold kept his forces under arms. They were based on the Isle of Wight, and the soldiers weren't grumbling – it wasn't a bad life, spending the summer months by the sea, with little to do except amuse themselves and scan the horizon for an enemy who showed no sign of turning up. Harold kept the Fyrd for two months longer than their normal stint, and it is a sign of his great popularity that he was able to do so without too many grumbles.

But by September, the soldiers were needed at home. The harvest had to be brought in. Each village required all the help it could get to ensure there was enough food to keep everyone alive through the winter. Harold thought it safe to send the Fyrd home. He didn't think that William would set sail so late in the year, risking the autumn storms.

Then bad news came from the north. Tostig had joined forced with Harald Hardrada, the gigantic, ferocious King of Norway, and together they invaded Yorkshire. William had helped this invasion by sending Tostig sixty ships. William hoped in this way to weaken Harold's rule and keep him busy with one set of invaders while he set about launching an invasion of his own.

All through the Summer, William had held regular meetings with his most important advisers. He was delighted when Cardinal Hildebrand (later Pope Gregory VII) and Abbot Lanfranc (later Archbishop of Canterbury) declared Harold a perjurer – that is, an oathbreaker, a liar. The support of these senior churchmen was vital for William.

Despite the approach of autumn, William and his fleet put to sea on 27th September. He had with him the Papal banner, symbol of the fact that the church supported his claim. He had also the ring of St Peter, and the holy relics over which Harold had been made to swear loyalty.

Mathilda gave William a ship as a good-luck present. The ship was called the *Mora*, which may have been William's affectionate nickname for Mathilda. Like the other Norman ships, the *Mora* was of square-rigged Viking design. At her prow was a carved lion's head, at her stern the figure of a child holding a horn and pointing towards England.

William had troops of about seven thousand men at his command. The ships had to carry everything – men, weapons, horses, food, fresh water, tools and prebuilt wooden walls so that they could quickly build a fort where they landed. The ships had flaming torches attached to their masts so they could keep track of each other at night.

Neither William nor anyone else knew exactly where they would land. There were several ports along the south coast of England, including Hastings. William was probably heading for Winchelsea, but he, like all sailors of his time, was at the mercy of the wind and waves. Halfway across the Channel the ships became separated by the wind. The *Mora* outdistanced the others, but William refused to panic. He ordered the sails to be furled and an elaborate breakfast including spiced wine to be served while he waited for the other ships to catch up.

***

When Harold heard news of the invasion of Tostig and Harald Hardrada up in the North, he was struck down by the paralysis that had crippled him before. Never had he more need of his physical strength, and here he lay, helpless in bed! Was this a sign of God's displeasure, a message that he was not, after all, the rightful King of England? Earlier, in the spring, a comet had blazed across the heavens, its fiery tail streaming. People had taken this as a bad omen, a sign that disaster was to befall. Had these doom-sayers been right?

But God had worked a miracle for Harold before; he prayed that this would happen again. He prayed as hard as he knew how. Sure enough, the afflicted leg grew stronger. Harold made a superhuman effort, summoned his troops, and set off on the long journey up Ermine Street, the great Roman road that led to the North of England. Harold's men on their little horses trotted through the villages, blowing their horns, enrolling the Fyrd; the women and children crowded to their cottage doorways to watch them go by, their hearts filled with a mixture of excitement and alarm.

The riders were followed by the foot soldiers; most of the Fyrd were on foot. It was an heroic march. They reached York, entered in proud procession through the Eastergate to the cheers of the townsfolk, and pressed on to confront Tostig and Harald Hardrada at Stamford Bridge, seven miles east of the city.

There were troops of about ten thousand on each side – armies the size of the entire population of London were fighting in this remote spot. No one had seen such a tremendous battle before. Snorri, a Norwegian maker of sagas, wrote that Harold's army "looked like a sheet of ice when the weapons glittered."

The two sides were well matched. Harald Hardrada was the most feared man in Europe. His name meant "hard bargainer", and his banner, showing a black raven on a white background, was known as the "Land Ravager". He was now 50 years old, and ever since his youth he had lived a life of greed and violence. Once, laying siege to a city, he had been taken ill, and had turned rumours of his illness to his advantage. He had staged a mock funeral; his followers had carried his (empty) coffin to the city gates and begged to be allowed in so that they could give their leader a Christian burial. The priests of the city had let them in. Immediately the bearers dropped the coffin and blown the call for attack. Harald, fully recovered, had led his men in massacring the citizens and ransacking the churches.

Then there was the time when Harald Hardrada was imprisoned by the Byzantine Empress for swindling. He escaped down a rope, blinded her husband, abducted her niece, rowed a galley across a chain blocking the Golden Gate – the exit from Byzantium– collected his treasure and married the daughter of the King of Novgorod. Yes, the Norwegian King was a force to be reckoned with, and now, as old age loomed, he threw all his prodigious strength into what would be his last chance to grab the throne of England.

King Harold Godwinson disguised himself as a herald and set out to meet Tostig before the battle began. "What will my brother give Harald Hardrada for his trouble?" asked Tostig, unaware that it was his brother he was talking to.

"Somewhat about six feet of English soil," Harold replied, "or perhaps a jot more as Hardrada is such a big fellow." He meant, of course, that there could be no truce, that he would fight Hardrada to the death.

And that is what happened. The English army fought the invaders fiercely in hand-to-hand combat, and at last the colossal Hardrada fell, pierced in the neck. Tostig, too, was slain, falling in the fading light and swirling mists of evening. The bloodshed had been tremendous. For years and years afterwards, the bones of the fallen were turned up by farmers' ploughs.

Harold rode back to York in triumph. But he was given no time to relax and relish the taste of victory. He organised a celebratory feast, but then he received the terrible news that William's fleet had landed at Pevensey in Sussex. There was not a moment to be lost. Harold rallied his tired troops and set off on the long march south.

At Waltham, near Epping Forest, he stopped to visit the abbey he had founded when his first attack of paralysis had been miraculously cured. Here he rededicated his life to the Holy Rood and beseeched God's support in the ordeal that lay ahead. He took leave of Edith Swanneshals, his loving companion for so many years. Would he ever see her or their five children again?

Though he had won the Battle of Stamford Bridge, he had suffered considerable losses. He had few archers left, his housecarls had been reduced by nearly half, and all his men were exhausted. He sent a herald on ahead to summon the Fyrds of Kent and Sussex to meet him at the hoary apple tree on Caldbec Hill, about six miles inland from Hastings. He had been told that William's invading troops had laid waste to his manors near Hastings, and he was livid with rage.

Harold and his men made the march south in record time. They hoped to surprise the Normans with the speed of their advance. The English soldiers spent the night of the 13th-14th October close by the hoary apple tree; Harold ordered that they should stay fully armed, but at nine the following morning he received a terrible shock. There stood the enemy assembled on Telham Hill, scarcely a mile away, ready for action.

***

When the Norman fleet had landed at Pevensey, William, in his eagerness, had stumbled and fallen forward on the stony beach. His followers gasped in consternation – surely this was an unlucky omen? But William characteristically turned a bad moment to his advantage. Grasping handfuls of pebbles, he raised them aloft. "See, how I seize the kingdom of England with both hands!"

The Norman soldiers set about making a fort, using the materials they'd brought with them on their boats. William's discipline was strict. Soldiers in those days robbed and intimidated the local population wherever they found themselves, but William forbade any looting until he gave the command. A few soldiers had died on the voyage, but William ordered that these deaths be kept secret, for fear of disheartening the living. And, once all his ships had landed, he ordered that holes be made in the bottom of each one. He didn't want the faint-hearted to think they could slip away in the ships and slink back to Normandy. By holing the ships, he was letting the men know that they had no choice but to stay on and fight the English – to the death, if need be.

Now William had to decide what to do next. He had no map to guide him, and he knew little about the terrain in which he found himself. He sent scouts riding out to find out more. They reported a densely wooded landscape, with lot of little hills and valleys, fertile and well watered, not heavily populated but scattered with villages and small towns.

News travelled slowly in 1066. No message could be brought more quickly than at the speed of a galloping horse. So when William landed in England, he didn't know what had happened to the Northern invasion. He didn't know who he'd be fighting – Harold Godwinson, or Harald Hardrada. He didn't know the whereabouts of either army. He decided not to move too far away from the coast. If he advanced a long way into England, there was a danger that he would be cut off.

He marched to Hastings, about ten miles from Pevensey. Here he built another temporary fort. Now, he gave his men the order to plunder the land. They seized food, tools, money and weapons from the villagers, and often set fire to buildings and ransacked storage barns as well. This was partly to give the soldiers the supplies they needed, partly to terrify the English peasantry into submitting to the rule of a foreigner, and partly to anger Harold – if he was still alive.

Eventually, news arrived of Harold's victory at Stamford Bridge, and of his march south. The two leaders exchanged messages. Harold said that God should judge the justice of the rival claims through a single battle between the two armies. William said there was no dispute between the two peoples, so he challenged Harold to hand-to-hand combat. William was banking on his immense physical strength, on the fact that he was a little younger than Harold, and on the fact that Harold would still be exhausted after his hard march south. But Harold decided to venture all upon his personal popularity and leadership skills; he insisted on a full-scale battle. Gytha, Harold's mother, pleaded with him to reconsider, but he would not.

Outwardly, Harold was fierce and brave, but inside, he felt sure that his last hour had come. The unease that had been growing within him ever since the appearance of Halley's comet now seemed to fill his whole mind. Everywhere William went, he showed off the Papal banner, St Peter's ring, and the holy relics over which Harold had been tricked into swearing loyalty. The Pope, head of the church, God's representative on earth, was on the side of William. This mattered a lot to Harold. He wouldn't admit it, even to his closest companions, but he felt that he was doomed.

When Harold saw the enemy gathered, waiting for him, on Telham Hill, he decided on a defensive strategy. He kept his men close together, high on a ridge. He hoped the Normans would not be able to penetrate the English shield wall. But the men on the ridge were too squashed; there wasn't enough room for manoeuvre. They couldn't defend the ridge and launch an effective attack on the Normans. And the Norman cavalry was a new terror. The Battle of Hastings was the first battle ever fought on English soil with a large number of mounted soldiers.

When William was preparing for battle, he put his chain mail on back to front. Once again, some of his followers saw this as an ill omen, but William brushed aside such superstitions. God would decide the issue, he declared – details were unimportant.

The battle was ferocious and lasted all day. William fought as fiercely as any of his men. Each time his horse was killed under him he sprang up in search of a fresh mount. At one point a rumour ran through the ranks that William had been killed; the soldiers' nerve was weakened. William, careless of personal danger, pulled off his helmet, so that all could see he was alive. His men cheered, and renewed their efforts.

Norman arrows rained down on the Saxons, who had lost many of their archers at Stamford Bridge. An arrow struck King Harold in the eye. Staggering, clutching his face, he knew he had no chance now. He had barely time to mutter a last, hasty prayer as the blades of the Norman axes bit into his back.

Once their king was dead, the Saxons gave up. Some fled into the surrounding forest, but were pursued by the Normans. The sickly stench of blood hung over the battlefield; everywhere, severed limbs and the corpses of horses lay scattered. Years later, the monks of Battle Abbey said that the name for this area, Senlac, came from the French for "Lake of

Blood", and that when it rained the earth wept blood. This legend probably arose because the soil in East Sussex is rich in iron ore, which gives the streams a rusty orange colour.

Harold's body was hacked into pieces and horribly mutilated. A knight, thinking to please William, presented him with one of Harold's legs, but William disowned him for dishonouring the corpse. Harold's mother pleaded with William and offered its weight in gold to be allowed to give the body a Christian burial. Poor Gytha! She had suffered the loss of four of her sons in three weeks, first Tostig at Stamford

Bridge, and now Leofwine and Gyrth, along with Harold, had been slain at the Battle of Hastings. Edith Swanneshals identified the body parts, and they were gathered together, but William refused Gytha's request. Instead, he had them wrapped in a purple cloth and buried under a pile of stones on a cliff top near Hastings. A companion of Harold's called William Malet, who was half-English and half-Norman, was given the grisly task. Malet put up a gravestone on which was written: "By command of the Duke, you rest here a King, O Harold, that you may be guardian still of the shore and sea."

Later William was to relent. The remains were disinterred, and buried properly, with the full rites of the church, at Waltham Abbey, as Harold would have wished.

William allowed the English to search for and bury their own dead. For days after the fight, the battlefield was crawling with people looking for the bodies of friends or relatives, or hunting for jewels, coins, weapons – anything of value. The proud regiment of housecarls was gone for ever. Hardly any of them survived the Battle of Hastings. The power of the famous Godwin family was also destroyed for good. What remained of Harold's family disappeared into obscurity.

William kept his troops at Hastings for a week after the battle, to regain their strength. Then he moved them slowly round southern England, imposing themselves on the native population. He burned the towns of Dover and Southwark and laid waste the surrounding countryside. The English could be in no doubt that the Normans were a force to be reckoned with.

They marched through Sussex, Kent and Surrey. William sent detachments to Winchester, the most important city after London, to ensure its surrender and that of Queen Edith, widow of Edward the Confessor and sister of Harold. At last, William and his army crossed the Thames at Wallingford and entered London.

On Christmas Day, 1066, in Westminster Abbey, the newly-consecrated church which had been restored and rebuilt by Edward the Confessor, Duke William of Normandy was crowned King William of England. William was a conqueror indeed.

Chapter Five
Edith Swan-neck

" There was one person who m Harold's death hit particularly hard. On the day of the battle, Edith Swan-neck had waited anxiously for news of her love.

"Come, Mother. We will learn nothing tonight. I'll watch with you again at first light." Edith started at the sound of her daughter's voice. She had been sitting for hours on the bench by the entrance to the manor house, watching for a messenger. She turned to look at Emma, aware of the stiffness in her chilled joints. I'm not as young as I was, she thought. The best of my life is over.

Emma stood silhouetted in the doorway, lit from behind by the fire that still blazed in the middle of the hall, despite the lateness of the hour. Edith had ordered that the fire be stoked high, kept blazing all night long. How could she sleep – how could the household sleep – until there was news of Harold, King of England, lord of this manor, father of Edith's five children, and her husband in the eyes of theworld if not in the eyes of the church? This Northerner he'd lately married, this Ealdgyth; Edith didn't waste time thinking about her. It was a purely political marriage. Edith knew that she alone had Harold's heart.

Emma was well-grown, straight-backed, at fifteen already a woman. She had her father's thick yellow hair; she wore it plaited in a rope that reached below her waist. And she had inherited her mother's grace-ful neck, that had given Edith the admiring nickname of Swanneshals. Emma had the look of a princess – as I did, thought Edith, and for a moment she saw her young self in her daughter.

The years melted away, and she was a girl again, at the time when she had first caught Harold Godwinson's eye. Harold was feasting in the great hall of her childhood home. "Bring spiced wine for our visitor," her father had commanded and she had brought it, warmed, in the silver goblet with the handles fashioned like crouching lions that they reserved for honoured guests. She had coiled her fine, fair hair and pinned it to the top of her head. She felt the young warrior's eyes upon her, admiring her, drinking her in.

"And this is your daughter?" Harold had said to his host. "May I ask her name?"

"Edith is her given name, but all about here do call her Swan-neck."

"Such a name is well-deserved." And as Harold drank deep of the rich wine, his eyes met hers over the rim of the goblet, and before she could look away in maidenly modesty her heart was lost.

And now here was Emma, just the age she had been then! Today's events at Hastings would decide her fate. If Harold was victorious, Emma, his wealthy, beautiful daughter, could make a fine match, perhaps even marry into royalty. But if Harold was defeated, Emma and her brothers and sisters faced a future of poverty, obscurity and mortal danger.

Edith's heart tightened with anxiety for her children. She rose. Emma was right, there would be no messenger so late in the evening. The mild October day had turned cold. Evening mists hung like wraiths between the trees and the ferns that coiled about her bench looked black and damp. In the surrounding woods, owls called as they went about their secret business. In the stables, the horses sighed and shifted and rustled their straw. Something – a rat or a toad – scuttled across Edith's path, so close it touched the hem of her robe. She pulled her cloak more closely about her shoulders and went inside.

Edith's maid rose from her place beside the fire, but Edith waved her away. "Hilda, go and rest. Tonight, Emma shall attend to me." Emma followed her mother into the chamber where they both slept, unless Harold was paying one of his all-too-infrequent visits, in which case Emma slept with Hilda and the other maids. Emma preferred the goosedown softness of her mother's bed to the prickly straw-stuffed pallets the servants used, but she enjoyed the gossip of the maids'chamber, the giggles and whispers that continued long after the tapers had been extinguished.

Edith seated herself by the oaken table on which stood her mirror of burnished steel – a present from Harold, plundered from a Danish ship. It was the only mirror in the house; everyone else looked at their reflections in the duckpond, if at all. Emma fixed two lighted tapers on either side of the mirror. The dim reflection made her mother's face look soft and young. She unpinned Edith's hair and combed it out so that it rippled like water. In this twilight, it looked as lustrous as the hair of a young girl.

Edith reached for her daughter's hand. Somehow it felt easier to speak to her reflection in the mirror than to address her face to face. "My daughter," she said, "My heart is heavy with foreboding. If this should be your father's last battle, remember him with honour, for he was a valiant man."

"Oh mother, don't say such things! There is no news. Why should you talk of my father as if he was dead and gone? Not three weeks since he defeated Hardrada – he cut the invaders down like grass. Why should he not deal the same to these Frenchmen? I have faith."

Edith's smile was sad. "You have the faith and hope of youth, Emma. But the last night your father was here – which I fear was the last night I will ever spend in his arms, though I pray for it to be otherwise – he told me that the omens were against him. Everywhere William the invader goes, he flaunts the banner of the Pope, and the holy relics with which he once tricked Harold."

"Those things are but toys, mother! God will see that justice is done. I cannot believe that my father –" but she stopped, because the unmistakable clatter of hooves rang out in the yard. In the mirror, the eyes of mother and daughter met for a split second that both would remember for the rest of their lives. Then Edith ran to the door.

The noise had woken the servants; a little crowd had gathered. Edith ordered the great door to be unbarred. The rider had dismounted; the stable boy ran out to lead his tired horse to the drinking trough. Edith recognised the messenger – Wulf, one of Harold's housecarls, a man she could trust.

Wulf looked at the lovely woman in the fireglow, her fair hair cascading over her shoulders, and his heart smote him. He fell to his knees before her.

"It is over," she said, before he had spoken. It was more a statement than a question.

"My lady, all is lost. My lord lies slain, may God have mercy on his soul." He made the sign of the cross. "I wish with all my heart that I could bring you comfort, but there is none to give. The King's brothers perished also, and I, almost alone among the housecarls, escaped with my life."

The servants broke into noisy weeping, but Edith remained calm. "Wulf, I thank you for telling me the truth." She turned to the servants. "Bring this man food and drink, and find him a warm place by the fire. But tell me, Wulf, where does the King lie? I must go to him, and that right speedily."

"My lady, I have a message for you. Be not angry, that it comes from our enemy. Duke William granted me safe passage, if I would ask you to come to the battlefield and seek out the King's body. Such is the carnage that his remains cannot be recognised, unless by one who – who – "

" – knew him and loved him as I did? Poor Wulf, how you must have dreaded delivering this message!

But of course I will go. It is the last service I can perform for my lord. I will depart at first light."

"And I with you, good lady. When my horse and I have fed and rested, we are yours to command."

"So be it. I thank you." Edith turned to Emma. The girl's face was as white as moonlight, and her eyes glittered with unshed tears. "My daughter, you must manage all here while I am gone. I will travel with Wulf, and with some monks from Waltham Abbey to support me – will someone go, now, and rouse Brother Gregory and Brother John?" One of the manservants rose to do her bidding. She placed a kiss on Emma's high, pale forehead.

"I see by your face that this night you have left your childhood behind you. I am glad you do not try to stop me. I think you understand that this journey I now undertake is my last great act of love."

***

It was the stench of the battlefield that stayed with Edith. Every sense was assaulted – the sight of the piles of bodies, men and horses hacked to pieces or twisted into horrifying shapes; the hooded forms of the living stooping over the corpses; some mourners like herself seeking the remains of husbands, lovers, sons, so that they might be given an honourable burial; others looters, plundering the corpses for weapons, jewels, purses, anything they could strip or wrench away. And the sounds – the heart-stretching wails of the bereaved; the buzzing of flies, wakened from their autumn sleep by the promise of a gory feast. As she bent to touch the bodies, searching for

Harold's, the damp chill of dead flesh made Edith shudder. But it was the sickly smell of blood that

seemed to invade her whole being, so thick that she could taste it at the back of her throat.

It was hard work, turning over the corpses, looking for clues that would lead her to the man with whom she had shared her life so gladly, so joyously. Wulf was by her side; he worked without cease, despite his bitter day's fighting and his hard ride from the battlefield to Waltham Manor and back. Brother John and Brother Gregory, monks from Harold's foundation of Waltham Abbey, gave her courage with their prayers and chants.

Two of Duke William's men searched with them. These two had been fighting near the spot where Harold had fallen when the arrow pierced his eye. Duke William had had audience with Edith. She had not understood his Norman French, nor he her guttural Anglo-Saxon, but his demeanour had been grave, respectful. The interpreter conveyed the Duke's desire to give Harold a hero's burial. Edith suppressed her doubts; she had no choice but to trust him.

Now the Norman knights indicated by their gestures that they were as close to the spot as possible.

Looters had worked all through the night, stripping the bodies as systematically as ants, and with as little feeling. Most of the corpses were now naked, their chain mail and leather jerkins gone. Edith knew that the Normans had mutilated Harold, hacking off head and limbs. She had tried to prepare herself. But still, when she found him, the shock ran through her like a lightning strike.

His torso was flung over the flank of a dead horse, in just the attitude she had so often seen him stretched out upon the pillows of their bed, lost in sleep. She knew it was him, because there on his stomach, just below his navel, was the cluster of brown moles that reminded her of a pattern of stars. And there on his chest was the ridged scar that bore witness to a fight he'd had as a young man – not a battle scar, but the stern reminder of a foolish squabble over a game of dice. How well she knew these marks on his body! How many times she had planted kisses upon them, sworn that she loved every inch of him, scars and all!

But oh, the horror. One arm was missing completely, the other dangled, nerveless, crossed with gashes. Both legs were hacked off at the knee. And the head was gone. Edith had longed to look at his face one last time, bloody and blinded though it would be.

There on the sticky, flattened grass she knelt and paid homage to what was left. She pressed her face to his cold chest and held him in her arms. Wulf and the monks stood by, their heads bowed. Even the Norman knights were silent and still. Edith's voice was a whispered sob. "I've found you, my love. And now I must bid you farewell."

She held him for a while. In her mind she was back in the days of her youth, holding him close in the long grass on the riverbank, listening to the light breeze stirring the reeds and the sound of his breathing, so warm, so close. Then she rallied herself, placed one last kiss on the chill flesh, and rose.

CHAPTER SIX
LAW AND ORDER

William had won the Battle of Hastings and had himself crowned King of England, but he was generally feared and mistrusted. Very few Englishmen welcomed his arrival. In the early years of his reign, he was kept busy controlling rebellions all over the country.

William was a strong, effective ruler because he acted with unbending insistence on his own authority. His ideals were: to keep peace within his own lands, to do justice firmly, to punish wrongdoers, and to protect the church. And he needed to persuade the English that his conquest was legitimate, that he was the rightful heir to the throne.

He had rivals right from the start. As soon as the news of Harold's death reached London, the elders of the City of London elected a fourteen-year-old named Edgar the Æthling, as King. William didn't regard young Edgar as a serious threat. He incorporated him into his court, and took him to Normandy when he returned there for a visit in the spring of 1067. Lots of other English noblemen went too. The Normans marvelled at their blond hair and at the strange language they spoke. At this stage William was trying to learn English, but he soon gave up, and reverted to Norman French.

William heard mass every day. He ordered that every soldier who had killed someone at the Battle of Hastings should do a year's penance for each victim slain. For his own atonement, he sent huge amounts of English treasure and money to more than a thousand Norman and French churches. He sent Harold's war banner to the Pope, to thank him for his support. And – perhaps in fulfilment of a vow he'd made before the battle – he founded Battle Abbey, which was built on the spot where Harold fell. The Abbey had something of the purpose of a modern war memorial, a reminder of the courage of those who gave their lives.

William took religion very seriously. When, in 1074, he was admitted to the co-fraternity of the Norman Abbey of Cluny, he told his barons that he saw this as "a pledge of eternal salvation, far greater than gaining the crown". He enthusiastically supported measures to insist on the celibacy of the clergy – that is, rules that didn't allow priests to have wives or girlfriends – and he ran an orderly and moral court. He was shocked and disgusted by the licentious behaviour of his own son, Robert.

William understood how important ceremonies and displays were in establishing his power. He introduced the "laudes regiae" – ritual chants that were sung during mass at important religious festivals. The chants spoke of the glory and importance of the King. They were a dramatic statement of William's place in the hierarchy of heavenly and earthly powers. At Christmas, Easter and Whitsun there would be a "crown-wearing", a huge cathedral service at which William would wear his crown and other regalia.

One Christmas, William was camping in the ruins of York after having crushed a rebellion, but even there he insisted on having his crown and robes brought to him all the way from Winchester so that he could still hold a crown-wearing ceremony.

William's Norman followers only amounted to 25,000 people, a tiny number compared to the Saxon population of about two million. The Normans had to make their presence felt. Not only did William have to stamp his authority on the rebels in this new kingdom, he also had to maintain order back home in Normandy.

He held his lands together by constant travelling – throughout his reign, he was rarely in one place for more than a few weeks. He also relied on a well-organised system of communications, and he knew how to display his authority so as to strike fear and admiration into his subjects' hearts.

He replaced most of the English aristocracy with his Norman henchmen, and redistributed their lands. Similarly, the leading English churchmen were replaced by Normans. To several of his closest friends he granted large estates in Sussex, so that the lines of communication between England and Normandy could be kept open.

With each block of land came a castle. Castle-building was vital in making the newcomers feel secure. Many Norman castles can still be seen nowadays, and we can imagine how grim and threatening they must have looked to the Saxon peasants. Norman castles consisted of a motte – a mound of earth – on top of which was a wooden tower surrounded by a plastered fence called a palisade. Below this was the bailey, or courtyard, containing the hall, chapel, barn and stables. The bailey was surrounded by another palisade and a ditch. People entered by the drawbridge, which could be pulled up to keep enemies out. If attackers did manage to get over the drawbridge, then the defenders would hurry to the motte and take refuge in the tower, demolishing the stairway behind them. The castles belonging to the most important noblemen were built out of stone, and it is these that have survived. The most famous is the White Tower, now part of the Tower of London, which was built from pale stone brought over from William's favourite town of Caen.

Before long, an Englishman couldn't go far without seeing some potent symbol of Norman power — a castle, a high wall to protect a garrison, or a grand new church. People became familiar with the image of King William on coins or on the royal seal which gave dignity to legal documents. And before long, Norman power began to seep into the English consciousness in more subtle ways.

The Norman conquest had a greater effect on the English language than any other historical event.

Within a few years, 85 per cent of the Old English vocabulary was lost. Indeed, for a long time it seemed unlikely that the English language would survive at all. Not one of the great new landowners spoke English. French words to do with military affairs took over, and these are the words we still use today, for instance "army" (armée), "soldier" (soudier) and "guard"(garde). So did words describing the social order – "crown" (corune), "duke" (duc), "nobility" (nobilité) and "peasant" (paisant). And our legal vocabulary also comes from Norman French – "judge" (juge), "jury" (juree), "gaol" (gaiole), and "accuse" (accuser). King Harold was the last English-speaking King of England, the last to take his oath in English, for three hundred years.

William encouraged marriages between the Normans and the Saxons, the conquerors and the conquered. He wanted to make the Norman presence in England feel normal; he wanted his kingship to seem part of the natural order. In the long run he succeeded, but he had a lot of trouble controlling the rebels first.

After the Battle of Hastings, Gytha, Harold's

mother, had taken refuge at Exeter, surrounded by her supporters. Early in 1068 William's army besieged the city. He had a hostage blinded within view of the city walls, to terrify the rebels into surrender, but they bravely held out for another nineteen days. When at last Exeter fell to the Normans, William gave lenient terms to the defeated. He wanted to show off his power, but he also wanted to reassure people that, under his rule, life could return to normal. Soon after the siege, Mathilda travelled to England, and was crowned Queen on 11th May. This was an important sign to the English that William and his family were here to stay.

Meanwhile, young Edgar the Æthling slipped away from court and travelled to Scotland where he persuaded the Scottish King Malcolm IV to support his cause. The Northern earls Edwin and Morcar also rebelled against William's rule. William and his troops marched swiftly north. When the soldiers reached York, the rebels knew they were beaten. This expedition resulted in a great extension of William's power in the north of England.

The rebels laid low for a while, but they soon

found a powerful ally in King Svein Estrithsson of Denmark, who thought he had a claim to the English throne. The Danes set sail in 240 ships, and in the summer of 1069 they landed on the banks of the River Humber where they were joined by the English troops led by Edgar the Æthling. William's men encircled them, cutting off supplies. A truce was made – the Danes said they would return peacefully to Denmark in the spring in exchange for money, and permission to forage for supplies along the coast.

Some of the English rebels then took to the hills and planned further attacks. William divided his army into small units who pursued the rebels, slaughtered peasants, burned crops in store, and destroyed tools, ploughs and animals. Infected corpses were left decaying in their houses. Survivors were reduced to eating cats and dogs, or selling themselves into slavery. No inhabited village was left in the 65 miles between York and Durham, and the land remained unploughed for nine years. William's pitiless policy, called "the harrying of the North" was designed to ensure that the North Country could not support a rebellion in the foreseeable future.

Early in 1070 there was another uprising on the Welsh border. William was certainly getting to know the far corners of his kingdom very well! As usual, he led by example, putting up with hardship and discomfort, and using his huge strength to help lesser mortals over difficult terrain.

The Danes broke their promise; they didn't go home in the spring. Strengthened by the arrival of King Svein, they sent a division to the Isle of Ely (now part of Cambridgeshire) to join the last pocket of English resistance, which was led by a Lincolnshire thegn called Hereward the Wake. Earl Edwin had been betrayed and killed by some of his own men, but Morcar joined Hereward. William blockaded Ely with ships to the north and troops on all other sides. He built a two-mile causeway so that he could attack the isle from the west. Hereward the Wake escaped, but Morcar was captured, and put in prison for the rest of his life. The captured rebels were blinded and mutilated as an awful warning to others.

By 1072, William had established such control that he felt able to leave England in the hands of his deputies Bishop Odo and William fitz Osbern, and spend more time in Normandy. For the rest of his reign, he spent more time in Normandy than in England.

But when he was in England, the King loved to hunt. He created the New Forest in Hampshire for his own amusement. Many churches were destroyed and many people were evicted from their homes in order to turn that area into good hunting ground. Later writers pointed to the fact that two of William's four sons (Richard and William) were killed in accidents in the New Forest, and claimed that this was a sign of God's displeasure at what William had done to the region.

"He preserved the harts and the boars, and loved the stags as much as if he were their father," said one chronicler, but of course William preserved them only in order to kill them. He introduced strict laws against poaching; blinding was the penalty for killing a deer without permission. But many peasants, desperately short of food, still took the risk.

William wanted to establish himself as a strict but fair lawgiver. He set up the "land pleas", for example, which meant that grievances over land ownership could be given a fair hearing. This measure was taken to stop the Norman takeover of English land from collapsing into chaos. The chroniclers of the time criticised William's harshness, but they admired the strength of his rule. The *Anglo-Saxon Chronicle* comments that during William's reign, "Any honest man could travel without injury with his bosom [pocket] full of gold."

Soon, English and Normans alike came to rely on William for upholding law and order in both countries. As Bishop Lanfranc wrote to Pope Alexander II in 1072, "While the King lives we have peace of a kind, but after his death we expect to have neither peace nor any other benefit."

Chapter Seven
Trouble and Strife

In the earlier part of his reign as King of England, most of William's troubles came from outside – from the northern rebels and the Danish attempts at invasion. In later years, many troubles came from inside, from within William's own family.

For years, William had clashed with Robert, his oldest son. William had appointed Robert as heir to the Duchy of Normandy, but he often teased and undermined him in public. Unlike his father, Robert was short, and William nicknamed him "Curt-hose" which means "Short-trousers". No young man likes to be belittled by his father, and

Robert seethed with resentment.

William had more serious objections, too. He was an austere, self-controlled man, respectful of religion, faithful to his wife, and uninterested in excessive drinking or gambling, though he did enjoy feasting and towards the end of his life became very fat. Robert, by contrast, was a party animal. He was popular amongst young men of his own age, and he surrounded himself with low-life characters, comedians, clowns, and prostitutes of both sexes. Wherever Robert went there was drunkenness and revelry. He was extravagant with money and with promises; he was forever offering ridiculous rewards to those who would support him.

All this did not bode well for Robert's future role as Duke of Normandy. William tried to control him by keeping him short of money and limiting his responsibilities. But Robert became bored and restless under this regime. "You treat me like a hired soldier," he complained to his father.

The crisis came in 1078. Robert's younger brothers, William Rufus, and Henry, were occupying the upper storey of a friend's castle in Normandy.

Several of Rufus' friends were with them, playing practical jokes and messing about. Henry, who was only nine years old, must have felt excited but perhaps a little nervous to be in such laddish company.

Robert Curthose arrived on horseback, also with a group of friends. When the lads at the top of the castle heard the clatter of hooves in the courtyard below, they leaned over the wall, calling out insults, and drenched Robert and his friends with water. Robert was furious. He stormed upstairs, and a huge row broke out.

William hurried to the castle to patch up the quarrel. He, too, was furious. He was a busy man — why should he waste his time on such trivial matters? Robert pretended to make peace, but the next night he and his friends deserted from the army and tried to storm the castle at Rouen. Their aim was to take control of the Duchy of Normandy. This would be Robert's by right after William's death, but Robert was sick of waiting. He wanted power now.

They failed to take Rouen castle — they were spotted by a vigilant castellan, who raised the alarm. So they fled to the frontier lands, where they were welcomed by William's enemies in the neighbouring states. Most importantly, Robert gained the support of King Philip of France. Robert occupied the castle of Gerberoi, waiting for his chance to lead an army against his father.

In January 1079 William besieged the castle of Gerberoi. The siege lasted three weeks and the fighting was bitter – William had his horse shot under him. Robert fought his own father and wounded him in the hand. Because of the chain mail and the helmet, Robert didn't realise who he was fighting until he heard his father's familiar harsh, gruff voice. William Rufus, who supported his father, was also wounded.

At length, an uneasy truce was established. William offered a money settlement to King Philip, who accepted it. After much discussion, peace terms were formally declared in 1080, confirming Robert's status as heir of Normandy. Pope Gregory VII sent Robert a letter reminding him of his duties as a son.

All seemed well again. But much damage had been done. The Norman aristocracy had been divided by the quarrel; there was distrust now, between those who had supported William and those who had favoured Robert. William's enemies had seen a chink in his armour and it had given them hope – the King wasn't as all-powerful as he made out. And the whole business caused the first serious rift between William and Mathilda. Mathilda loved her eldest son dearly, and had been terribly upset by the fact that he could not get on with either his father or his brothers. She secretly sent money and messages to Robert. When William found out, his rage was terrifying.

Robert wasn't the only family member to incur the King's displeasure. For years, William had relied on Bishop Odo, his half-brother, who had always supported him, and had been richly rewarded for doing so with money, titles and lands. Odo acted as William's deputy in England when the King was in Normandy. Odo was a clever man with two sides to his character. He did much good for the town of Bayeux, where he was bishop. He built a new cathedral, provided grants for young scholars to continue their studies, and, above all, commissioned the magnificent Bayeux Tapestry which told, in embroidery, the story of William's conquest of England. The Bayeux Tapestry is one of the most important pieces of historical story-telling that survives, and it is certainly one of the most beautiful. It was made in England, and probably displayed at the dedication of Odo's new cathedral in Bayeux on 14th July, 1077.

But, though he was a generous patron of education and the arts, Odo was also a forceful character, greedy and ambitious. He was hated and feared by the peasants on his English estates; one chronicler described him as "a ravening wolf". While William was detained in Normandy by the trouble with Robert, Odo enjoyed a long period of being in control in England. He wanted greater, more lasting power for himself.

He became involved in a scheme to make himself Pope. He bought a palace in Rome, and bribed leading Romans to support his bid for the papacy. William strongly disapproved of this behaviour. He objected to Odo's arrogance, and claimed that he was taking much-needed knights away from England. Late in 1082 he captured Odo and imprisoned him at Rouen.

Odo's political career was over, and so was all possibility of friendship with William. With Odo removed from the scene, William came to rely more and more on his other half-brother, Robert of Mortain. When eventually William died, Robert of Mortain was the only close family member who was present.

William had other troubles besides family ones in these later years of his reign. His traditional enemies in France, who had lain low for some time, now revived themselves, inspired by the feud with Robert, and William had to suppress raids along the frontiers of Normandy. And there was continuing instability along the northern and western fringes of his English kingdom. In 1075 there was a revolt led by the Earl of Norfolk and Suffolk and the Earl of Hereford, who enlisted the support of the Danes. William returned from Normandy to England to deal with the Danes. They didn't dare fight him, but returned to Denmark with their ships laden with treasure after yet again sacking York.

The rebellion was suppressed and as usual the rebels were punished. Amongst the victims was Earl Waltheof of Northumbria, who was beheaded. Many people criticised William for allowing this execution to happen. There was little or no evidence, they said, to show that Waltheof was a traitor. Before long, miracles allegedly started to occur at Waltheof's tomb. People began to revere him as a martyr. Orderic the historian pointed out that, after Waltheof's execution, William never again drove an army from the field of battle nor succeeded in storming any fortress which he besieged.

In 1079, the Peace of Abernethy – a truce between England and Scotland – collapsed, and the Scots King Malcolm raided Northern England. William trusted Robert enough to send him north with an army to fight Malcolm, and this expedition was reasonably successful. In 1081 there was more trouble in Southern Maine. But it is worth noting that all the troubles of 1076-81 took place beyond the frontiers of Normandy, in contrast to the troubles before 1060. William was still feared and revered. Apart from Robert, no one dared to attack him on home territory.

The triumph of the years immediately after the Conquest had been slightly tarnished, but the outlook was not all bad. William was still the strongest ruler in Europe. Despite piling on weight, he was healthy and active, and as keen a huntsman as ever. And his marriage survived the feud with Robert. When Mathilda died, on 2nd November, 1083, William buried her in splendour at her abbey of La Trinité, Caen, to which she bequeathed her crown, sceptre and other treasures. William built her a monument of gold and precious stones – it has gone now, but her tombstone can still be seen. William was deeply distressed by her death, and wept for days and days. Some suggested that he should marry again, but he could hardly bear to look at another woman, and remained single for the rest of his life.

Chapter Eight
Domesday and Doomsday

William had been King of England for nearly twenty years. He wanted to put a seal on his authority, to make some kind of statement that the Norman conquest of England was complete, and would not be reversed. During a crown-wearing ceremony at Gloucester at Christmas, 1085, an idea came to him.

He would have a survey made of all the counties of England. Everything would be listed – every building, every farm, even every farm animal. The survey would be made into a book, and then the entire wealth of England would be set down for all to see.

It would give him a clear picture of his people and his lands, and it would create a strong sense of order and structure for the English themselves. Though William was a skilled and fearless warrior, he did not seek war for the sake of it. He knew that peace was best. He wanted his England to be a peaceful, orderly country with a fair legal system and effective local government.

A huge team of information collectors was quickly organised. They worked in pairs – one man to ask the questions, the other, the "scribe", to write down the answers. They went into every town and village, and asked the inhabitants about their property. Then the information was all written out by a single scribe and bound together in what is called the "Domesday Book".

There are actually two books, Great Domesday and Little Domesday. Great Domesday surveys all the counties south of the River Tees, except for Norfolk, Suffolk and Essex – these three are surveyed in Little Domesday. North of the Tees, William's control was still not strong enough to allow a reliable survey to be carried out. The English counties as described in

Domesday remained more or less the same until major boundary changes were made in 1974.

The *Anglo-Saxon Chronicle* says, "So very narrowly did he [William] have it investigated, that there was no single hide nor a yard of land, nor indeed... one ox nor one cow nor one pig was there left out, and not put down in his record." Nothing like the Domesday project had ever been carried out before, and the fact that he brought it into being shows what a far-thinking man William was. The Domesday book is an invaluable document for historians. Without it, we would know very little about life in the eleventh century.

Domesday was made with remarkable speed. The decision to do it was taken at Christmas 1085, and the whole thing was finished by autumn 1086 at the latest. In fact, it is likely that the records were presented to William on 1st August, 1086, at Old Sarum, now Salisbury, where a new town was growing up round the Norman cathedral. The *Anglo-Saxon Chronicle* tells us:

"And there his counsellors came to him, and all the people occupying land who were of any account over all England... And they all submitted to him and became his vassals, and swore oaths of allegiance to him, that they would be loyal to him against all other men."

Domesday could not have been carried out had William not felt certain of his position. He still had his troubles, to be sure. After Mathilda's death, he once more quarrelled with Robert Curthose. Robert was exiled from Normandy, and spent the next few years making his way round the coasts of Europe trying to get support from various kings, dukes and counts. And in 1084 William had to raise a huge "Danegeld" – six shillings for every hide – so that he could afford to billet his army throughout England, for fear of another attempted invasion from Denmark. William ravaged the coastline to make landing unattractive to the Danes. Then the Danish king, Cnut IV, was murdered while at prayer, and the threat dissolved. But aside from these problems, William's power was secure.

In the autumn of 1086, William left England for Normandy, taking lots of English money with him, to marry his daughter Constance to the Duke of Brittany. He did not know it, but this was to be the last time he crossed the Channel. He spent several months in Normandy; and then in July he laid claim to the region called the Vexin. He forced entry into the town of Mantes; his horse tried to leap a ditch and, in so doing, the hard, high pummel of the saddle was driven into William's stomach.

William became very ill. He ordered a retreat. He was carried to the priory of St Gervais at Rouen where he lay on what seemed increasingly likely to be his deathbed. William's mind remained clear. His internal injuries gave him great pain, and at first he panicked at the thought of death, but with a huge effort he got his fear under control. He was surrounded by clergy, some of whom were also doctors, and at various times by his sons William and Henry, his brother Robert of Mortain, and other noblemen. He made gifts to churches for the good of his soul and to win God's favour for his final judgement.

William agreed that on his death all his political prisoners should be released except for his now-hated brother Odo. But Robert of Mortain persuaded him to change his mind, and Odo was released. When William knew his end was near, he ordered Rufus to hurry to England, taking with him a sealed letter for Lanfranc, Archbishop of Canterbury. In the letter, William ordered Lanfranc to receive Rufus as King of England. William knew that the more quickly Rufus was proclaimed king, the better, before other claimants had a chance to muscle in.

William died at dawn on 9th September. His attendants looted his chamber, making off with everything of value. News of his death caused panic amongst the citizens of Rouen, who reeled about as if drunk. Norman aristocrats fortified their estates.

Everyone expected chaos now the great man was dead.

Between the hours of prime and terce – the old Latin names for six in the morning and noon – William's body lay abandoned. Everyone had respected William, but few had felt any affection for him. Now, nobody wanted to take responsibility for his body. At last an insignificant knight called Herluin agreed to take on the cost of embalming the body, which was carried by ship to Caen, because William wanted to be buried there in his abbey of St Etîenne. A procession followed the corpse through the streets of Caen, but when fire broke out in the crowded row of houses there was a general stampede. Only a few monks were brave enough to carry the dead king to his last resting place.

The only one of William's sons to be present at the funeral was Henry. The body lay on a bier in the middle of the church for all to see. The Bishop of Caen gave an address, but then there was a disruption as a man named Ascelin stood up and declared that the land on which the church was built had been wrongfully taken by William from Arthur, his father. There was much hasty conferring. It was decided that Ascelin's claim was just, and he was offered money in compensation.

The time had come to lower the body into the tomb. But William was a big man, and the hole that had been dug was too small. When the monks crammed the body in, it burst, releasing a revolting smell that no amount of incense could disguise.

***

William had none of the frailties that make a character sympathetic, but he was clever, clear-sighted and extremely courageous. Since 1066, England has never fallen to foreign invaders, and before long the Normans ceased to be invaders and became essentially English.

Robert Curthose was a disaster as Duke of Normandy. He couldn't control the rebellions all around him; during his reign, Norman authority collapsed. He ended his days as a prisoner of his younger brother Henry. William Rufus didn't do much better. He was corrupt and dissolute, and most people thought it was a good thing for England when he was killed by an arrow – an accident, or deliberate murder? – while hunting in the New Forest.

Rufus had no children, so Henry came to the throne. Of all William's sons, Henry was the most impressive. He had studied hard as a boy, so he was much better educated than his father. He delighted the English people by marrying a girl who was descended from King Alfred the Great. Like his father, he saw that marriage between the Normans and the English was a good way to help the two peoples to live at peace with each other. Henry also changed many laws to make them fairer to the English.

By the end of Henry's thirty-five year reign, the enmity between the invaders and the invaded had all but disappeared. Henry had completed his father's work. If William could have foreseen that all his hard work was to bear such fruit, nothing would have given him greater satisfaction.

CHAPTER SEVEN
THE CORONATION

Christmas night, 1120. The servants of the royal household and their families are gathered round the fire. Younger children are already asleep in their truckle beds or lolling on their parents' laps, but Steven is ten years old, and he is allowed to stay up to listen to the stories the adults have to tell.

They crack filberts and walnuts and sip from the steaming goblets into which Steven's mother ladles mulled ale from a cauldron where little brown crabapples bob like a shoal of fish. On Christmas Day here at the court at Westminster, the royal household feasts well. King Henry sees to that. There are hogs roasted on spits; tall, straight-sided pies fashioned like castles and stuffed with chopped meat, dried figs and plums; grilled quail; rabbits stewed with cinnamon and ginger; girdle cakes yellow with saffron.

Now the feast is over; tall hounds roam the hall, crunching on bones and licking grease and spilled gravy from the floor. The thick trenchers of bread that are used as plates have been doled out to the hungry beggars at the gates, along with some small coins; Christmas is a time for giving as well as feasting.

Steven's family have a long and proud history of royal service. His great-grandfather was one of King William's bodyguards, way back when the Conqueror was still only Duke of Normandy and the throne of England a distant dream. Steven's grandfather, Guy, was page to Duke William, grew up in his service, and became his valet – few could have claimed to know the great William as well as he. Guy's son Edmund, Steven's father, had a head for figures, and in his position as purser – or keeper of accounts – had reached almost the top of the pecking order in the royal household. And now young Steven was to begin his own training in the New Year, as page boy to King Henry, William's son.

Steven looks at the faces of his family, ruddy in the firelight. They don't often have the leisure to sit together like this and tell stories. Grandfather Guy is an old man now, with hardly a hair on his head, but his voice is still strong, and his wits are as sharp as ever. Steven enjoys the tales the adults tell of ghosts and strange happenings, of changelings left by the fairies in place of real babies, of giants and talking horses and fish that granted wishes. But tonight he wants a story from real life, and his grandfather has promised that he shall have one.

"I'm going to tell you about this day 54 years ago," old Guy begins, sure of his authority, confident that his audience will listen with respect. "Christmas Day, the year of our Lord 1066. I was page to Duke William, and just such a likely lad as our young Steven here. We didn't come over to England with the fleet – no, we youngsters were sent for once victory was assured. It was a terrible winter crossing; one of the ships went down, with my cousin Walter in it. The journey to London seemed never-ending, and how the people stared at us with their round blue eyes, muttering their gobbledegook! We Normans were a dark breed, you see, and I hadn't travelled before. It surprised me to see these yellow-haired Englanders with their red faces and long beards. They looked like bundles of hay that had come untied.

"Well, I'd been seasick, and now I was homesick. I longed to be back in Rouen, where everything was familiar. Pride was what kept me going – pride that I'd been chosen to attend to Duke William, or King William as he'd become. Preparations for his coronation were already under way, and we pages knew that we had an important job to do.

"We had a tutor to teach us the Saxon tongue. I learned quickly – you do at that age – and once I could make out what these shaggy blond ogres were saying to one another, they seemed less like ogres, and more like real people. I soon began to feel at home. King William tried to learn the language himself, but he couldn't take to it. He soon gave up. He had plenty else to occupy him, after all. But he was very keen that we should all mix with the locals. He promised a purse of gold coins to any of us who married an English girl. Well, I got my gold, didn't I, though not for a fair few years."

The old man pauses, and Steven knows he's thinking of Mildred, his wife, who died some years ago. Steven can only just remember his grandmother's smiling wrinkled face. He inches closer and leans his head against his grandfather's knee. Guy ruffles the boy's silky dark hair and continues his narrative.

"Where was I? Oh yes, the coronation. There was a lot of nervousness about that. It took place here at Westminster of course, in the Abbey, and it was the third big royal event there within the year, after King Edward's funeral and the crowning of Harold Godwinson back in January. And there were a lot of people – an awful lot of people – who didn't want to see a Norman on the English throne. So it was very important that we got it right.

"The King chose Christmas Day – well, what other day felt important enough? He chose the same rites, the same vows, that had been used to crown the other English kings. He wanted the English to accept him, you see. He wanted everyone to believe in his right to the throne. That's why he wanted us to marry English lasses – to smooth out the differences.

"He chose an English archbishop to crown him Ealdred of York, God rest his soul. He couldn't have Stigand of Canterbury. Stigand was the one who'd crowned Harold, that was fresh in people's minds, and besides, the Pope didn't like him. So Ealdred it was. He was a good man, and nobody's fool. He refused to crown William unless William swore on the Bible that he would govern the nation as well and as justly as the best of the kings before him, if the nation was faithful to him. So William swore, and that's more or less what came to pass.

"There were a fair few English bishops and abbots at the ceremony, as well as lots of French. They'd been summoned from the furthest corners of the kingdom – Herefordshire, Cornwall… The King respected the church all his life, and he wanted the church to respect him.

"So in went William in his great heavy robes, and after him followed us page boys, holding them up. We had on blue velvet tunics, midnight blue, with gold stitching on them, and our hose was yellow. The maids teased us about our 'chicken's legs', but we thought we looked mighty fine.

"The ceremony was long, and I couldn't understand the half of it, and the chanting of the monks and the incense from the censers that were swung the whole length of the abbey made my head spin. I was wondering how I could keep upright, when something happened that woke me up good and proper.

"The bishops had to call on the congregation to give their assent for the crowning to go ahead. First the call was in English, and the English present gave back their assent, clear but not loud. Then a Norman bishop – Geoffrey of Coutances, it was – called on the Normans to give their assent, and they shouted loud enough to raise the rafters.

"Now, my father was on guard outside the cathedral. Some of the guards were Normans, like him, and they understood what the shouting was about. But half the guards were Saxons, and they panicked. They heard all this hollering in a foreign tongue going on inside the abbey, and they thought there was a rebellion afoot. So they laid about them like crazed men, knocking people over the head and setting fire to houses, treating the crowds like they were an armed uprising instead of a bunch of ordinary folk who'd come along to pay their respects, or out of simple curiosity. My father tried to stop the torching, but they didn't understand him. And the next thing we knew, smoke from the burning houses was blowing back into the abbey.

"Half the congregation gathered up their robes and fled, like a flock of frightened geese. It was not a dignified sight. Archbishop Ealdred called for calm, but he could hardly be heard above the hubbub. He and the other clergy carried on and finished the ceremony, though some of them were trembling like willow leaves dangling over a brook in autumn.

"I looked at the other page boys – there were four of us – and we winked at one another. We stood firm. We hadn't made that terrible voyage over the stormy Channel to run away now. So we carried on as if nothing had happened.

"King William was trembling, too. He shook from head to foot. We pages talked about it later, when we were curled up in the bed we all four shared, like a litter of puppies.

"'Did you see the King shaking?' asked Hugh. 'He was afraid for his life.'

"'He wasn't shaking with fear,' said I.

"'What was it, then? A sudden ague?' Hugh's voice was sarcastic.

"'It was – excitement. King William doesn't know fear. Fighting's meat and drink to him.'

"'I agree', put in Charles. 'He trembled not like a coward, but like a war horse, pawing the ground ready for battle.'

"We talked about the end of the ceremony, when we'd all left the abbey and returned to court for our

Christmas feast. King William didn't overlook us. He laid his hand on each of our four heads and commended us for our courage. And, later, he had a ring made for each of us, in honour of the day."

The old man sits back and takes a gulp of ale – his throat is dry from so much talking.

"Is that the ring you wear still, Grandfather?" asks Steven, who knows the answer.

"Yes, indeed." Guy spreads his hand as best he can, hooked by arthritis as it is. On his little finger is a ring of dull gold, set with a flat agate bearing the King's crest.

"When he gave it me, it was too big, and I wore it on a chain round my neck. And now it's too small, and my flesh grows in ridges round it. But I've never parted with it, and I never shall. When I die, young Steven, it shall be passed on to you."

And I'll sit here, some Christmas night in years to come, thinks Steven. I'll tell the story of the ring to a grandson of my own. Steven looks at his little finger, and imagines the ring there, and the thought sends a shiver down his spine. Who'll be King of England then? There are some things nobody can know.

Timeline

1027/8	William born at Falaise, Normandy.
1035	Duke Robert, William's father, dies. William becomes Duke of Normandy.
1050	William marries Mathilda.
1051	Edward the Confessor nominates William as his heir.
1064	Harold is shipwrecked and taken prisoner in Normandy. He swears oath of allegiance to William.
1066	Jan 5th: Edward the Confessor dies. Spring: Halley's Comet appears and is seen as an omen. Sept 12th: William and his fleet put to sea. Sept 25th: Harold wins the Battle of Stamford Bridge. Oct 14th: William wins the Battle of Hastings. Christmas Day: William is crowned King of England in Westminster Abbey.

1068	May 11th: Mathilda crowned Queen of England.
1070	William defeats rebellion led by Hereward the Wake.
1077	July 14th: Bayeux Tapestry displayed at dedication of Bayeux Cathedral
1078-9	Robert Curthose tries to take control of Normandy, but fails.
1082	William and Odo quarrel. Odo imprisoned at Rouen.
1083	November 2nd: Mathilda dies.
1087	Domesday Book compiled.
	July: William is injured entering Nantes.
	September 9th: William dies. William Rufus becomes King of England.

QUIZ

After you've finished the book, test yourself and see how well you remember what you've read.

1. What did William's mother Herleva dream of when she was pregnant with him?

   That her child would be carried off in a hot-air balloon

   That her insides were stretched out over Normandy and England

   That the Normandy football team won the World Cup

2. William's father sent back from the Holy Land:

   St Catherine's wheel

   St Michael's underwear

   St Stephen's fingerbone

3. As a boy, William:

   Got 10 A* GCSEs

   Never went to school

   Was permanently excluded for threatening the teacher with his sword

4. How did William defeat the enemy at the Battle of Varaville?

   By attacking the rearguard when it became separated by the rising tide

   By disguising himself as a water-carrier and sneaking into

the enemy camp to steal their battle plans

By reducing them to helpless laughter with his funny stories

5. William's wife Mathilda was known for being:

Remarkably hairy

Grossly obese

Exceptionally short

6. Why was Edward, the King of England, called "The Confessor"?

Because he would always own up to his mistakes

Because of his deep interest in religion

Because he was a great fan of the heavy-metal band of that name

7. What was a "Danish marriage"?

An arrangement that allowed the husband to take another wife at a later date

A wedding at which a smorgasbord was served to guests

An elaborate kind of pastry formed of two interlocking spirals

8. After proclaiming, "May the Lord strike me down if I am guilty", Godwin promptly:

Choked to death on a fishbone

Slipped on a banana skin and broke his neck

Caught a particularly virulent form of athlete's foot which then spread all over his body

9. What were the names of Harold's brother and nephew who were held hostage in Normandy?

Wolfbroth and Chicken

Willywonka and Akorn

Wulfnoth and Hakon

10. Why did Harold build an abbey at Waltham Cross?

He thought that young men of the area would otherwise turn to a life of crime

He wanted to show his gratitude to God for curing him of paralysis of the leg

He needed a cover for training spies to infiltrate the Norman defences

11. What did Mathilda give William as a present as he set off to invade England?

A ship

A suicide pill

A week's-worth of clean underwear

12. Harold Hardrada's banner, which showed a black raven on a white background, was known as:

The Range Rover

The Road Runner

The Land Ravager

13. Where did Harold assemble his troops prior to the Battle of Hastings?

   The Olde English Tavern in Pevensey High Street

   The hoary apple tree on Caldbec Hill

   The junction of the A2101 and the A259

14. What did William do to show his troops that he had not been killed in battle?

   Pulled off his helmet

   Started to sing the Norman national anthem

   Sent them all a text message

15. What was the motte in a Norman castle?

   The mound on which the tower was built

   The ditch surrounding the castle walls

   The public toilet used by all inhabitants

16. Why was the New Forest created?

   So that William had a good place to go hunting

   To give the local population somewhere to go for a picnic at weekends

   In order to provide mushrooms for the new French restaurants that were springing up all over England

17. Why did William nickname his eldest son, Robert, "Short-trousers"?

    Because cropped trousers were very popular at the time and Robert was a great follower of fashion

    Because in reality Robert wore baggy flares

    Because Robert was not very tall

18. Bishop Odo wanted to:

    Change his name

    Become Pope

    Put embroidery on the National Curriculum

19. How long did it take for the Domesday Book to be compiled?

    Less than a year

    1-3 years

    More than a decade

20. What unfortunate incident happened at William's burial?

    His body burst open as it was being crammed into a tight grave

    No one came because they had been given the wrong date

    A herd of runaway cattle stampeded through the cemetery trampling the mourners and priests

Charlotte Moore has written two other books in the WHO WAS... series, *WHO WAS...Florence Nightingale: The Lady with the Lamp* and *WHO WAS... Elizabeth I: The Kingly Queen*. Her latest book *George and Sam,* tells of life with her two autistic sons. She is also the author of several novels.

She lives in East Sussex.

Other titles in the WHO WAS... series:

WILLIAM SHAKESPEARE
The Mystery of the World's Greatest Playwright
Rupert Christiansen

Everyone has heard of plays like *Macbeth* and *A Midsummer Night's Dream*. But why do we know so little about the man who wrote them? Who exactly was William Shakespeare from Stratford-upon-Avon, and why do so many people believe that he was not the person he seemed to be?

This book is an exciting detective story, which goes back over four hundred years to the dramatic events of the reign of Queen Elizabeth I and explores the way that a brilliant and ambitious young man was caught up in a violent world of murder, revenge and treason.

ISBN 1-904095-34-8

WOLFGANG AMADEUS MOZART
The Boy who made Music
Gill Hornby

By the time he was four years old, it was clear that Wolfgang Amadeus Mozart was a musical genius. He could already play the clavier, the organ and the violin to perfection.

When he was just seven, little Mozart began touring Europe, performing at court to kings and queens, and in concert halls to crowds of the paying public. His father could see that Wolfgang would one day change the face of European music, and presumed that the adult Mozart would be wealthy, famous and adored around the world. What he did not know was how hard it can be for a child genius to grow up...

ISBN 1-904-977-64-2

CHARLES DICKENS
The Man who Invented Christmas
Andrew Billen

Young Charles Dickens's happy childhood came to a sudden end when his father was jailed for debt and, aged 12, he was sent to work in a factory making shoe polish.

By his mid twenties, he was on the verge of becoming the most popular novelist the world has ever know, creating hundreds of unforgettable characters. But Charles never forgot his days working alongside poor and abandoned orphans.

Andrew Billen tells the gripping life story of Charles Dickens, explaining how it fed into his work. and how, along the way, he invented the modern idea of Christmas.

ISBN 1-904977-18-9

ISAMBARD KINGDOM BRUNEL

The Iron Man

Amanda Mitchison

From tunnels and railways to bridges and ships, Isambard Kingdom Brunel would stop at nothing to realise his amazing engineering idea.

Born at the beginning of the nineteenth century, Brunel had a brilliant brain for design, and never tired of building new and exciting things – the deepest tunnel, the longest bridge, the fastest train. For Brunel, the average and the ordinary were just not good enough. A perfectionist and a control freak, he would stop at nothing to complete a project, even when it meant taking hair-raising risks...

ISBN 1-904977-59-6

Dear Reader,

No matter how old you are, good books always leave you wanting to know more. If you have any questions you would like to ask the author, Charlotte Moore, about *William the Conqueror* please write to us at: SHORT BOOKS, 3A Exmouth House, Pine Street, London EC1R OJH

If you enjoyed this title, then you would probably enjoy others in the series. Why not click on our website for more information and see what the teachers are being told? www.shortbooks.co.uk

All the books in the WHO WAS… series are available from TBS, Distribution Centre, Colchester Road, Frating Green, Colchester, Essex CO7 7DW
(Tel: 01206 255800), at £4.99 + P&P.